SERVING
OTHERS
ALONG
THE ROAD

SERVING OTHERS ALONG THE ROAD

Revealing
Christ's Love
Through
Holiness

FRANK MOORE

The *Holy Life* Bible Study Series

BOOK 4

Beacon Hill Press of Kansas City
Kansas City, Missouri

Copyright 2004
by Frank Moore and
Beacon Hill Press of Kansas City

ISBN 083-412-128X

Printed in the
United States of America

Cover Design: Ted Ferguson

Library of Congress Cataloging-in-Publication Data

Moore, Frank, 1951-
    Serving others along the road : revealing Christ's love through holiness / Frank Moore.
        p. cm. — (The holy life Bible study series ; bk. 4)
    ISBN 0-8341-2128-X (pbk.)
    1. Holiness. 2. Holiness—Biblical teaching. I. Title II. Series: Moore, Frank, 1951- . Holy life Bible study series ; bk. 4.

    BT767.M675 2004
    248.4'071—dc22

                                                    2004003070

10 9 8 7 6 5 4 3 2 1

Contents

For the Group Leader

How to Use This Study Book

We trust that this study will be a valuable resource to you and others in helping you grow in holiness and Christlikeness. It is written and organized to be used as a small-group Bible study, with 12 weekly sessions. The following are some brief guidelines to help you maximize your group's time together.

1. Pray regularly throughout the week that your group sessions will be times of warm fellowship and genuine spiritual growth. Most of all, ask that the Holy Spirit will be present in a powerful way, speaking to and challenging each group member to a life of holiness. Open and close each weekly session in prayer.

2. Prepare well for each session. Carefully study the scripture readings and exposition prior to your group meeting, which will help you facilitate the discussions and keep them moving.

3. Use the group discussion questions and activities to promote lively dialog among group members. Feel free to contribute your own comments as well, but don't allow any one member of the group (including yourself) to dominate the discussions.

4. Whenever it's practical, link your own comments to those of others. Affirm each group member. This will help encourage some of the more reticent members of your group to participate in the discussions.

5. Respect the confidentiality of what is shared within the group.

6. Encourage group members to come to each session prepared, having studied the lesson and scriptures carefully, in addition to having meditated on the personal reflection questions.

7. Encourage any group member who has made any type of personal decision for Christ (salvation, sanctification, or

other) to make his or her decision public as soon as possible at one of your church's worship services.

In the World but Not of It

John 17:14-18

In Book 1 of this Bible study series, *God's Road Map for Us*, we looked at God's original plan for humanity, our rejection of that plan, and His efforts to get humanity back on track with the plan. In Book 2 of the series, *The Journey Within*, we looked at holiness from the perspective of individual believers. Book 3, *Traveling with Friends,* turned our attention to holiness as we live it in the Christian community and the world. We talked about a proper understanding of corporate faith as biblical Christians.

In Book 4 we look at another essential perspective for biblical holiness. We now focus on letting holiness lead us into ministry and service. Book 3 reminded us that we can't live a life of holiness in isolation but that holiness will lead individual believers to participate in the larger Christian community and the world. This participation in the world will include more than going out in public only when necessary—such as work or the grocery store. We'll study biblical passages that challenge us to purposefully go forth into our world with a commission from God himself.

I remember hearing of an ancient saying that goes something like this: "There are two wings by which we rise—personal piety and community charity. No one can fly by flapping only one wing." So true! The union of piety and service has been a hallmark of Holiness people throughout Church history. Even a quick read of the Church's story reveals a close connection between consecrated hearts being sanctified by God's Spirit and deep involvement in meeting the needs of hurting humanity. Let's turn to Scripture to see God's direction for our lives once He has established our hearts in holiness.

GROUP DISCUSSION

1. Give examples, either from your personal awareness or from Church history, of people who loved the Lord deeply who also heavily involved themselves in service to hurting humanity.

2. What have been some of the social causes holiness people have championed across the years?

3. Why do you think an experience of heart holiness leads so naturally to service and ministry involvement?

READ JOHN 17:14-15

In Book 2, Study 9, we learned how John saw spiritual matters in black and white. People either love God or they hate Him; they're for Him or they're against Him. Nobody gets to ride the fence. In Book 3, Study 6, John compared and contrasted the kingdom of God with the kingdom of Satan. Everyone belongs to one or the other; no third option exists. Now Jesus tells us the same thing. He contrasts His ways with the ways of the world and His Spirit with the spirit of the world. He warns us that we can expect to receive the same rejection and harsh treatment that the world gave Him. The world is likely to reject us just as it rejected Him.

If we stopped our reading at verse 14, we might assume permission from Jesus to take this gospel message of life and salvation and hide away with it, awaiting our transfer to heaven. But Jesus didn't stop there, and He didn't give us permission to hide. Far from it! Notice the charge in verse 15. He's leaving us right where we are—in the world. He prays for a wall of protection to shield us from the evil one, but we're left in the rough and tumble of the world nonetheless. Talk about a challenge! Jesus admits He's sending us into hostile territory. Then He aims us in the direction of a firestorm.

GROUP DISCUSSION

1. Why do you suppose both John and Jesus found it important to remind us of the sharp contrast between the kingdom of God and the kingdom of this world?

2. Why did Jesus make a special effort in His last quiet conversation with His disciples to warn them that they could expect to receive the same rejection and harsh treatment that the world gave Him?

3. Why is it natural for us to want to withdraw from the world that rejects Christ's value system?

4. Why does Jesus not give us the option to withdraw from the world?

READ JOHN 17:16-17

The language of verse 14 has Jesus comparing His disciples with himself. Verse 16 compares Jesus' disciples with the world. We won't fit into the world's reality any better than Jesus did, because something about both Him and us places us out of sync with the world. Jesus says we are to live *in* the world but not *of* it. What a powerful message in those two-letter words!

With this command Jesus instructs us to live fully in our society. We rub shoulders with the world every day at work, school, and play. The clothes we wear, the cars we drive, and the food we eat all mark us as participants in a particular society. However, even though we physically function in this environment, we're not of this world. That is, we don't adopt the world's value system or worldview. We don't think the way the world thinks; we don't adopt the world's agenda. We march to the beat of a different drummer.

We know the Spirit of God sanctifies us as a gift from His loving hand, as we studied in Book 2, Study 7. This sanctification involves separation both *from* something and *to* something. He separates us *from* the world and its life of sin; He separates us *to* a life of holy service. This sanctification affects every part of us: spirit, soul, and body. Jesus adds a new thought regarding our sanctification in verse 17. He tells us that God sanctifies us by His truth.

Obviously, believers live in an atmosphere of truth. They tell the truth and live transparent lives, opening themselves fully to the light of God's truth. More than that, however, Jesus indicates from the tone of this verse that our sanctification occurs with the aid of God's truth. This truth exposes the bankruptcy of sin, the flesh, and selfish lifestyle choices. It rips the glitter and glamour away from the costumes worn to Satan's parties to reveal the bondage, addiction, pain, suffering, and death that are the ultimate results of going the way of the world. God's truth reveals this reality to His children and separates them from these harmful results.

PERSONAL REFLECTION

1. In your own words explain how believers are to be in the world but not of it.

2. How has God's truth separated you from the value system and worldview of the world?

READ JOHN 17:18

In verse 18 we have our marching orders. Not only does Jesus not allow us to hide from the world as recluses while we wait on our transfer to heaven, but He sends us right back into this world that has rejected both Him and us. It seems that after the rough treatment the world has given us, Jesus would let us hide out at church or in each other's homes! No. He sanctifies our hearts with His truth and then turns us right back around with the challenge "Go back into your world and help people." That's a hard homework assignment. The fire in the fireplace warms so well. Fellowship with Jesus and other believers fulfills so completely. What could be better? God's will does not leave us in our cozy, warm, protected environment, though. He sends us out.

God does not forgive us of our sins and sanctify our hearts to place us on a fireplace mantle like a trophy. He cleans us up and screws our heads on straight so we can go out and offer His comfort. He doesn't comfort us to make us comfortable but to make us comforters. That's the message Jesus gives us in this week's scripture study. That's Paul's call as well in 2 Cor. 1:1-14. He speaks in verses 3-4 of "the God of all comfort, who comforts us in all our troubles, so that we can comfort those in any trouble with the comfort we ourselves have received from God."

That means we can't withdraw from society and form a counterculture. Christians have tried that strategy from time to time throughout Church history. They withdrew to the mountains, caves, or wilderness to create a separate environment totally isolated from society. But we can't be much good for God and His kingdom if we're off by ourselves praying and singing. So Jesus sends us out into our world, just as the Father sent Him into our world.

GROUP DISCUSSION

1. Why do you suppose the withdrawal plans of Christians to mountain, cave, or wilderness hideaways never worked very well for very long?

2. Why won't God let us stay in our warm, protected environments?

3. Does Jesus' challenge to us to go back into our world and serve excite or scare you? Why?

4. What does the following statement say to you? "God doesn't comfort us to make us comfortable but to make us comforters."

GROUP ACTIVITY

Divide the class into two groups. Have each group take one of the following sentences and complete it in various ways that support that particular mind-set. Share all responses with the entire class when ready.

1. Christians should withdraw from the world because . . .

2. Christians should go into the world to serve because . . .

FOR FURTHER STUDY

Gen. 28:15

John 15:3

John 1:10-13

FURTHER QUESTIONS

Take a moment at the conclusion of the session to encourage class participants to place their unanswered questions on note cards, along with this session number. They should then place their cards in an "odds and ends" box provided by the Bible study leader. Attention will be given to these questions in the last session of this study.

Salt, Light, Yeast

Matt. 5:13-16; 13:33

I've always been fascinated by the story of Abraham bargaining with God regarding judgment on the city of Sodom, recorded in Gen. 18:16-33. Our attention most often focuses on the wickedness of the city, or we conjecture concerning the particular sins that displeased God. Sometimes we even marvel at the boldness of Abraham because he had the nerve to enter into a bargaining session with the Almighty of the universe. I'm even more amazed at the fact that God fully engaged in the negotiating session. He's far more approachable than we realize.

I want to focus our attention on another angle of Abraham's divine encounter, however. Notice two things: righteous people strategically located in the city would spare it from God's judgment, and the number of people required was amazingly small. Bottom line—as few as 10 righteous people have enough spiritual influence to spare an entire city from judgment. Now, that's incredible. Jesus called attention to this in His ministry with His analogies of salt, light, and yeast. We hinted at the first two in Book 3, Study 7. Let's go for more detail this time.

GROUP DISCUSSION

1. What spiritual lessons do you learn from Abraham's divine encounter in Gen. 18:16-33?

2. What do you learn about God from this story?

3. What do you learn about the power of prayer from this story?

4. Why did Abraham have the nerve to keep dropping his number—from 50 to 45, then 40, then 30, then 20, and finally 10?

GROUP ACTIVITY

Contact three group members prior to the Bible study session. Have one bring a container of salt, another a flashlight or lamp, and the third a packet of yeast and a baked loaf of bread. Ask each to demonstrate the features of his or her object that have spiritual application. Allow class time for the three people to present their object lessons. Move from the lessons into a study of the text.

READ MATT. 5:13

What qualities of salt might Jesus have had in mind for His followers? I usually think of salt as having the following qualities.
- It has a unique flavor, different from that of any other food or spice.
- It preserves meat.
- It flavors other foods for richer enjoyment.
- It disinfects by killing germs.
- It makes people thirsty.

All of these qualities apply naturally to the spiritual effect Christ's followers have in the world. We should be different in outlook and perspective from the rest of the world based on the fact that we live and think by a different value system and worldview. We should act as a preservative the same way a few righteous inhabitants of Sodom could have preserved that city from judgment. We should add flavor in work and social settings by our positive and upbeat perspective on life. This perspective results from spending time with the Author of life. Our personal morals and ethics should be so clean and pure that the people who know us best know that we live above reproach. Our lives should have hidden qualities that make people thirst to know what makes us different and to want to be like us.

In biblical times salt lost its flavor by falling on the ground or being exposed to rain and sun. Like salt falling on the ground, we, too, can lose our spiritual dynamic by taking on bad habits of the world or getting caught up in worldly thinking. Like exposure to rain and sun, we can lose our spiritual dynamic by letting the natural stresses and strains of life get to us and simply wear us down. We can't allow either of these negative influences to sap us of our spiritual dynamic. As Jesus says, if we let that happen, we're good for nothing in terms of Kingdom building.

GROUP DISCUSSION

1. Give a practical example of each of the qualities of salt as applying to the Christian's life.

2. What threats pose the greatest danger in robbing believers of their spiritual dynamic?

READ MATT. 5:14-16

What qualities of light might Jesus have had in mind for His followers? I usually think of light as having the following qualities.

- It's not self-produced; it's reflected from a source.
- It reveals the road in front of us.
- It produces heat.
- It provides power.

As with salt, all of these qualities apply naturally to the spiritual effect Christ's followers have in the world. As believers, we never produce our own spiritual light; it always shines as a reflection of God's light. For this reason we refer to our holiness as a reflected holiness. The spiritual influence of believers should provide light on the road for those who don't know God personally. The wisdom of our counsel comes not from our keen insight but from time spent reading God's Word and talking with His Spirit. Our smiles and warm presence should comfort all who come in contact with us just as a fireplace warms all who stand near it. Our lives should exhibit a spiritual power explainable only by factoring in God's work in our lives.

Jesus calls attention to three spheres of influence for light: home, city, and world. A lamp's light reaches only one room of a private home. The light of an entire city can be seen for miles. The sun's light spreads across the whole world. A Christian's spiritual influence must begin in the home. From there it reaches the hometown and can spread across the world. We don't all have the same degree of influence. However, God expects us to be as effective as possible in doing the most good with the light we have to offer.

PERSONAL REFLECTION

1. In what way is your spiritual influence like light?

2. What are you doing to assure that you're as effective as possible in making the most of your light?

READ MATT. 13:33

Matt. 13:33 contains the only biblical reference to yeast that does not in some way compare it to the permeating spread of evil in our world. Here Jesus calls attention to the fact that a very small amount of something can have a powerful influence. He also reminds us of the quiet, seemingly unnoticed, impact of our influence.

I'm not handy in the kitchen. In fact, my wife, Sue, pretty well bans me from attempting a creative hand at cooking in her kitchen. I've proven myself a failure with that art! She does let me make bread in the bread maker, however. I'm always amazed at the small amount of yeast needed to influence an entire lump of bread dough. After the ingredients are mixed, the yeast needs several hours, a warm room, and just the right humidity to do its thing.

As followers of Christ, we must act like yeast in a lump of dough. It doesn't take too many of us to have a profound impact. Just look at the handful of followers in the Early Church. They took the entire Roman Empire by storm in less than 300 years. Most of the time our influence works quietly and seemingly unnoticed. But given the right conditions, our influence can be powerful, not because of *our* ability but because of the ability of the Spirit of God working through us. Never underestimate the power of yeast!

GROUP DISCUSSION

1. Think of an example of one Christian or a small group of Christians who made a powerful influence on society.

2. In what ways does a Christian's influence work quietly and unnoticed in society to bring about great good?

FOR FURTHER STUDY

1 Cor. 7:16

2 Cor. 9:2

1 Thess. 1:8

FURTHER QUESTIONS

Take a moment at the conclusion of the session to encourage class participants to place their unanswered questions on note cards, along with this session number. They should then place their cards in an "odds and ends" box provided by the Bible study leader. Attention will be given to these questions in the last session of this study.

Leave the Altar and Report to Work

Rom. 12:1

One night when I was about 12 years old I heard a strange noise coming from the woods behind our farmhouse. It sounded like an injured animal, and I had a hard time falling asleep as I lay in bed trying to pinpoint the source of the sound. The next morning I told my dad what I had heard. He had heard it too. I insisted he search through the woods to see if he could locate what we had heard. In an hour or so, he returned home with a beautiful but badly injured tan collie. He resembled Lassie, only he was a bit leaner. It seems a neighboring farmer set traps along the fence line that joined our farm to keep wild animals away from his livestock. This unsuspecting dog accidentally stepped into one of the traps.

We nursed the collie back to health and offered him a new home. We named him Lucky because of his good fortune in coming our way. Lucky and I bonded tightly. He became my best friend for the rest of his life. I know you won't believe me, but I think he remained forever grateful that my dad rescued him from the trap and gave him a new home. Lucky always had a look in his eye that said, "I'm never going to forget what you did for me." And he didn't. He spent the rest of his life right by my side.

What does Lucky's story have to do with this Bible study? It clearly illustrates the concept of a living sacrifice. He showed his gratitude for his rescue by spending the rest of his life serving faithfully at my side. He dedicated all his attention and energy to being my childhood companion.

GROUP DISCUSSION

1. Have you ever owned a pet that poured its life into serving you?

2. In what ways did your pet serve you?

3. Have you ever had friends, coworkers, or family members for whom you did a special favor that helped them so much they felt indebted to you?

4. How did it make you feel that they wanted to do something to pay you back for the way you helped them?

READ ROM. 12:1

We studied Rom. 12:1 in Book 2, Study 6. Our approach in that study focused on the theoretical message of our consecration to God: what it means and how we do it. We want to look at the passage again from a practical perspective this time. It's one thing to offer yourself to God's service; it's quite another to roll up your sleeves and get busy. Let's focus on the notion of a living sacrifice.

We're familiar with the practice of offering God a sacrifice. We studied the practices of the Old Testament sacrificial system in Book 1, Study 9. Offering sacrifices was central to worship throughout much of the Old Testament. Worshipers brought animals for the high priest to slay and lay before God on the altar. The animal's blood symbolized its life; the shedding of that blood reminded worshipers of the seriousness of their sins. The offering indicated to God that they truly wanted to please Him.

A dead sacrifice has very little earthly value. It lies on the altar as a statement to God and others of worshipers' religious intentions, but its service ends once its life ends. That makes the New Testament concept of living sacrifices far superior to the Old Testament concept of dead ones. A living sacrifice can actually do something.

GROUP DISCUSSION

1. What are the major messages God hoped to teach His people through the Old Testament sacrificial system?

2. Make a list of all the ways a living sacrifice is better than a dead one.

God calls us in the New Testament era to offer our living bodies. This contrasts the Old Testament offering of dead animal bodies. Our bodies have been filled with the life and energy of God's Spirit. We must use this divine gift of new life and energy to do God's service.

Paul's words remind us of Heb. 10:5-7, which is a quotation from Ps. 40:6-8. We're told of the Old Testament passage prophecies of the coming of Christ, who in turn makes this His testimony. Notice how Christ sees past the sacrifices and offerings of the Old Testament sacrificial system to the real offering worshipers should bring to God: a body dedicated to doing God's will.

God has literally delivered New Testament believers like us from the death grip of sin, addiction, and bondage. We used to abuse our bodies in selfish habits and practices that brought us fleeting moments of pleasure and satisfaction but left us empty and alone. We would regroup and abuse our bodies again in a week or so. We stumbled from one binding habit to another. None offered lasting meaning; none brought life. But God changed all that. He broke the death grip on us and restored us to life, health, and wholeness. He made our bodies into temples for His Holy Spirit (1 Cor. 6:19-20).

PERSONAL REFLECTION

1. Think back to the bondage of your old life of sin. Where was it leading you? Where would you have ended up if Christ had not rescued you?

2. In what ways did God bring you from death to life when He saved you?

3. How is Christ our example in offering our bodies to God's service?

The fact that Paul calls attention to our bodies reminds us that God calls us to more than lip service. This act of worship of which he speaks involves more than talking and singing. It requires giving our time and energy in the form of action. It puts feet to our words. It brings fulfillment to our lofty intentions.

It's so easy to get caught up in the thrill of a touching worship service. We sing at the top of our voices and pray from the depths of our soul. Nothing wrong with either, but you can't take that to the bank. In other words, they're just that—words. Paul calls us to take those well-intentioned words and follow them up with *deeds*. Worship begins in our hearts and works its way out into our bodies. Again, Christ serves as our example.

GROUP DISCUSSION

1. Which is easier—words or deeds?

2. Have you ever experienced a meaningful worship time with God in which you planned to do something tangible for the Lord, but then somehow you never got around to doing anything with your plan?

3. Why can good intentions be so frustrating to us?

4. How do you turn good intentions into actions?

Paul says presenting our bodies to God is a reasonable response. Old Testament worship services tended to be completely ceremonial. Everything from the priests' robes to the objects in the sanctuary spoke of formal ritual. Worshipers performed a prescribed ritual that, unfortunately, they could memorize and recite without thought. That's not a reasonable response to God.

Not only is our service reasonable from the perspective of good logic, but it also requires us to think about what we're doing. Paul urges us, then, to think about this service as we perform it, to replace ceremony and rote ritual with actions that flow from a heart devoted to showing God how much we love Him by the way we work hard for Him.

Taken together, this verse calls us, as those who have received new life from God, to lay ourselves on God's altar just as Old Testament worshipers laid sacrifices on the altars of the Tabernacle and Temple. We offer back to Him this new life He gives us. Just as my dog Lucky gave me that look in his eye, we give God a look that says, *I'm never going to forget what You did for me.*

GROUP ACTIVITY

Divide the class into two groups. Have group 1 list all the disadvantages of a dead sacrifice (and the limitations of the old sacrificial system). Have group 2 list all the advantages of a living sacrifice (and the advantages of God's new covenant with us.) Encourage each group to write its responses on a chalkboard or dry-erase board and share them with the entire class when ready.

FOR FURTHER STUDY

Heb. 10:5-7

1 Cor. 6:19-20

2 Tim. 2:21

FURTHER QUESTIONS

Take a moment at the conclusion of the session to encourage class participants to place their unanswered questions on note cards, along with this session number. They should then place their cards in an "odds and ends" box provided by the Bible study leader. Attention will be given to these questions in the last session of this study.

Taking Risks for God

Matt. 13:44-46

Folklore often circulates about buried treasure in secret locations or shipwrecks that carry great wealth to the bottom of the ocean. A story circulated through our extended family about the previous owners of our farm. The story says that about the time of the Civil War a man placed all of his family's material wealth in a wooden box and buried it somewhere on the property. He then died before telling anyone where he hid it. My sister, brothers, and I used to calculate where we might look for it. We even dug a few holes here and there to try our luck. We didn't find it!

In this week's Bible study, Jesus tells two such stories of hidden treasure. We're looking at these stories not so much to study the narratives themselves but to learn about the mindset that we believers must employ to focus on one purpose in life—a purpose to which we wholly dedicate ourselves.

GROUP DISCUSSION

1. Have you ever won a drawing, door prize, or sweepstakes of any kind? If not, have you known someone who did?

2. How did that make you (or your friend) feel?

3. Have you ever located an especially good bargain while shopping?

4. How did you feel when you realized you were getting a great deal?

READ MATT. 13:44

Matthew is the only Gospel writer to report the story found in 13:44. So more than likely, Jesus told the story privately to His disciples. He was giving them a special insight into Kingdom truths. Let's look at the main features of the story. First, we see that the treasure had been purposefully placed in this hidden location for safekeeping. Next we see that the man happened onto the hidden treasure by accident. He had not spent days sweeping the ground with a metal detector looking for it. He just stumbled onto the worthy find. Finally, we see that the man valued this treasure so highly that he sold every material possession he owned in order to purchase the land that held the prize.

What is Jesus telling us about God's kingdom in this story? First, He wants us to know that God has purposefully placed knowledge of His kingdom within our reach. He didn't drop it out of His briefcase by accident. God places awareness of His kingdom across our paths so we'll find it. Next, Jesus reminds us that our discovery of God's kingdom often appears to happen through a unique chain of events. Most of us have a story to tell of God's quiet providence leading us to Him. Finally, He wants us to recognize the incredible value of this prize. It's worth more than anything else in our lives. So we should stop wasting time and energy on all other ventures and focus our attention solely on giving ourselves to God's kingdom.

GROUP DISCUSSION

1. Why is it important to remember that God left the treasure for us and that we didn't find it by ourselves?

2. Why is it important to remember that our salvation came through a unique chain of providential events?

3. Our study of holiness in Book 2 taught us the importance of a single purpose in life—God's will. How does Jesus' parable illustrate this truth?

READ MATT. 13:45

Matthew is the only Gospel writer to report the story in verse 45 as well. This illustration differs slightly from the last one in order to highlight new truth. Whereas the previous man found the treasure by accident, this man found his prize while looking for it. The pearl merchant bought and sold pearls every day. He knew the shape, color, and size of a valuable pearl when he saw it. So every day he searched for that one special pearl—that find of a lifetime. Then one day he hit the jackpot! His lifetime of searching had paid off. He moved quickly, selling everything he owned to buy the valued prize. His actions mirrored the man in the previous story.

What new truth does Jesus illustrate? God's kingdom holds highest value not just for those who seemingly stumble onto it; it also rates highest among those who search for it. The life story of Saul of Tarsus (Acts 9:1-18) reveals the truth of the first parable. He found God's kingdom when he really wasn't looking for it. The life story of John the disciple reveals the truth of the second parable. He openly sought God's kingdom and immediately followed Jesus when called (Matt. 4:21).

GROUP DISCUSSION

1. Do you know anyone who sought for spiritual truth before discovering God's kingdom?

2. How does this life experience differ from one who finds God's kingdom seemingly by accident?

3. Should the level of commitment in the lives of those who stumble onto God's truth differ from those who find it by searching for it?

CONCLUSION

Both of these stories urge us to adopt the mind-set of a casino gambler! What? Have I lost my mind? Here's my logic. I've always been fascinated with the way casino gamblers think. They have great faith in their good luck. They believe hidden laws of the universe line up for a limited period of time to favor them. They believe so strongly in their good fortune that they're willing to bet their last dime on one roll of the dice.

Jesus urges us in these two stories to have faith in God and His kingdom. He has a whole set of spiritual laws that work in our lives when we join this kingdom. These laws work not just for a limited period of time but for all eternity.

We should believe so strongly in God's kingdom that we focus every ounce of our energy, every minute of every day, and every dime that comes our way on our investment in it. Christ's followers must not diversify. That is, we must not spread ourselves across a variety of efforts. We must single-mindedly pursue God's kingdom with all of our hearts, souls, minds, and strength. That's the mind-set of service and ministry holiness.

GROUP ACTIVITY

Have the Bible study leader interview a participant who has had opportunity to prepare beforehand and who is willing to share from his or her personal spiritual journey. The leader will ask interview-type questions that explore a time when this person took a risk for God. This exercise aims not so much to call attention to one individual's experience as to get all class members to examine their own lives and respond to God's invitation to venture out for Him.

PERSONAL REFLECTION

1. List all the efforts to which Christians often give themselves.

2. List the efforts to which you give yourself.

3. Which of these efforts would you need to drop if you focused more completely on pursuing God's kingdom with all of your heart, soul, mind, and strength?

4. The title of this week's Bible study is "Taking Risks for God." What risks have you already taken in your life for God?

5. What risks has God been calling you to take for Him?

6. In what ways might your focused efforts for God's kingdom be similar to those of a gambler?

FOR FURTHER STUDY

Luke 12:33

Phil. 3:8

John 18:36

1 Tim. 6:19

FURTHER QUESTIONS

Take a moment at the conclusion of the session to encourage class participants to place their unanswered questions on note cards, along with this session number. They should then place their cards in an "odds and ends" box provided by the Bible study leader. Attention will be given to these questions in the last session of this study.

A Lifestyle of Service

2 Cor. 11:23-33; 12:7-10

A young man named Brian participated in three Work and Witness trips to third world countries while attending our university. As a result of his experiences and God's call, he's now a career missionary. Fred felt directed to enter the field of medicine. That choice led him to move his family halfway across the country and go to medical school for several years. Eldon and Mary heard God's call. They quit their jobs, sold most of their possessions, and went to Africa.

My career as a college professor has brought me in contact with thousands of college students over the past two decades. I've watched students make decisions about courses of study, careers, mates, and lifestyles. Some have been wise choices, others not. One thing's for sure: the choices we make in crucial areas of life often have long-term consequences. I've seen my students choose paths at graduation that set the course for the rest of their lives.

Paul reminds us in the passages of Scripture we consider in this week's study that choices have consequences. Rather than going through these texts verse by verse or phrase by phrase, as we usually do, I want us to consider these passages in terms of the big pictures of what's being presented. Paul met Christ on the Damascus Road (Acts 9:1-9). He became a lifelong disciple, committing himself to wholly following the will of God for his life. As a result of that choice, Paul found himself in many less-than-desirable circumstances. However, he willingly endured those circumstances because they followed from his choice.

PERSONAL REFLECTION

1. Think of choices you have made in your life that have had long-term consequences.

2. Did you willingly accept the consequences that followed the choices? Why or why not?

3. Should we attempt to anticipate the consequences of our choices before we make them?

READ 2 COR. 11:23-33

In answering his critics, Paul gives us a bit of his remarkable biography. Read quickly back through 2 Cor. 11:23-33. Notice the key thoughts: hard work, prison, floggings with a whip, beatings with a rod, stonings, shipwrecks, being adrift at sea, being on the move, river crossings, bandits, enemies, labor, toil, insomnia, hunger, thirst, exposure to cold, nakedness, and escape from death plots. A good reference Bible will give you cross-references to read more on some of Paul's experiences recorded in the New Testament.

This list of events in Paul's life sounds like a list of things we might want to avoid. I mean, who wants a lifestyle that offers these kinds of events on a regular basis? Paul doesn't present this brief biographical sketch to brag or seek pity but rather, as he says in verses 30-31, to offer praise to God for meeting him at the point of his weakness with strength to endure. Paul illustrates in living color what a mind-set of service and ministry holiness looks like. God stationed Paul strategically in the thick of the battle, but He equipped him with what he needed for that assignment as well.

Paul reminds us that serving God does not promise a flower-lined path of ease. However, following Him in radical discipleship produces a great sense of fulfillment and satisfaction that words can't describe. Granted, the satisfaction we feel may be in the midst of extremely trying circumstances. Part of the cost of following Christ, as He urges us to do in Luke 14:26-35, is to come to terms with the fact that God's call on our lives may require extreme dedication and sacrifice. A heart totally sold out to God recognizes that and stands ready to meet the cost.

GROUP DISCUSSION

1. What are some of the ways Christ's disciples experience hardship for His cause today?

2. Why does God not deliver us from all of these hardships since we're serving Him?

3. How could Paul recount such misadventures without anger or resentment at God for allowing him to experience them?

4. Why does a mind-set of service and ministry holiness require total dedication?

PERSONAL REFLECTION

Think back over your own life. What has the cost of discipleship with Christ meant for you?

READ 2 COR. 12:7-8

Paul teaches one of the key principles of service and ministry holiness in 2 Cor. 12:7-8. That is, in the midst of very difficult circumstances, such as what Paul described in the previous passage, we can experience the blessing of God to the point that we wouldn't want life to be any other way. Paul does not suffer from delusions or denial; he's fully aware of the difficulty of his circumstances. In fact, he prays adamantly for God to remove some of his difficulties. Rather than removing the difficulties, God promises Paul an extra measure of grace.

Paul reminds us in verse 7 that, as strange as it sounds, these difficulties can actually be seen as gifts that God allows. God is not the primary giver of the difficulties—Satan gets that credit. However, God finds ways to bless Paul in spite of Satan's best efforts to defeat him. We have no idea what Paul's thorn might have been. Bible scholars have surmised answers for centuries without certainty. Pinpointing the thorn serves no purpose. We know the wide variety thorns come in, because we all have one or more of them. They're all different; they frustrate us equally regardless of the names they go by. They remind us, as they reminded Paul, that we're flawed earthen vessels as we discussed in Book 3, Study 3. They humble us and keep us dependent upon God.

The word Paul uses for "torment" in verse 7 actually means to crucify. As we identify with Christ's dying on the Cross for our sins, we crucify the passions and desires of our fleshly or selfish nature while we live in a mind-set of holiness. The thorns of life sometimes torment us as we live for

Christ on this earth. When they do, we make sure that everything but God's will for us remains dead.

GROUP DISCUSSION

1. Recount a time in your life when you experienced the
   blessing of God during a difficult circumstance to the point
   that your heart felt peace in the midst of the difficulty.

2. Why does God not always remove the obstacles from our
   paths?

3. What lessons can we learn from such difficulties?

4. How does this mind-set relate to service and ministry holiness?

READ 2 COR. 12:9-10

Paul teaches one of the key mysteries of service and ministry holiness in 2 Cor. 12:9-10. What a paradox! That is,
God's power sometimes works best in our lives at the point
of our greatest weakness. We may prefer not to have the
weakness, but somehow God's light may shine brightest
through it. If so, our openness to His will and plan for our
lives allows us to embrace even weakness.

Why did Paul endure the weakness, insults, hardships, per-
secution, and difficulties? For the sake of Christ! That's a very

good motivation for us to endure as well. Paul restates the paradox of verse 9 with a principle for life: "When I am weak, then I am strong" (v. 10). Paul says much the same thing in 2 Cor. 4:7—"We have this treasure in jars of clay to show that this all-surpassing power is from God and not from us."

GROUP ACTIVITY

Give every class member four Post-it notes. Ask each of them to think of two principles from this Bible study about difficulties in life and two principles about God's grace. They are to write these principles on their Post-it notes. Write "Difficulties in Life" and "God's Grace" in big letters on a chalkboard or dry-erase board. Have class members place their Post-it notes under the appropriate headings. Read all responses and discuss them. Highlight principles of service and ministry holiness.

FOR FURTHER STUDY

Phil. 4:13

1 Cor. 2:3-5

1 Pet. 4:12-19

FURTHER QUESTIONS

Take a moment at the conclusion of the session to encourage class participants to place their unanswered questions on note cards, along with this session number. They should then place their cards in an "odds and ends" box provided by the Bible study leader. Attention will be given to these questions in the last session of this study.

Keeping a Light Touch

Matt. 19:16-22

Dan was a student in two of my classes at the university where I teach. He was a good student with a sensitive heart toward spiritual matters. I don't know where he is today; I've lost touch with him. Dan quit school, disillusioned about Christianity as a result of his particular interpretation of the story from the life of Jesus found in Matt. 19:16-22. Dan interpreted Jesus' words so literally in this encounter that he believed Jesus disapproved of Christians earning money or owning any material items.

I tried to reason with Dan regarding the deeper meaning Jesus intended with these words, but he refused to hear them. Since I, along with every other professing Christian Dan knew, had a job that paid a salary, Dan reasoned that none of us truly followed Christ. So obviously none of us could be Christians. Like the man in this story, Dan walked away sad.

GROUP DISCUSSION

1. Do you know an individual or group of people who for spiritual reasons disapprove of the ownership of material items?

2. Why might people reason that material possessions harm spiritual progress?

GROUP ACTIVITY

Group leader: give every Bible study participant a small piece of red construction paper. Tell class members to interrupt you by waving their red flags every time you make an incorrect statement in your presentation. If they interrupt your lecture, they must then correct the incorrect statement. Then, as you make your Bible study presentation, purposefully make mistakes to see if class members correct you. If they miss something important, stop and correct yourself. This activity will keep everyone listening and make participation lively.

READ MATT. 19:16-20

Mark (10:17-30) and Luke (18:18-30) also relate Jesus' encounter with the rich young man, so we gather several insights about him from the three accounts. His unusual spirituality and material wealth had obviously earned him a high reputation at an early age. Unlike the Pharisees, who asked Jesus questions in hopes of tricking Him, the young man approached Jesus with the pure intention of asking an honest question. His spiritual sensitivity led him to a religious puzzle that he needed solved.

Religious teaching in Jesus' day claimed that God granted eternal life based on the satisfactory performance of particular religious or benevolent acts. This attitude still receives much attention today. The average person on the street will tell you that a place in heaven is earned via God's favorable judgment of our outward actions. Various lists of essential religious and benevolent acts circulated in Jesus' day. We discussed three such acts in Book 3, Study 9. The young man in this story wanted to be sure he followed the right list to assure eternal life. He recognized Jesus' authority and wanted to get His final word on the subject.

Jesus pointed him to the Ten Commandments. His reference to the One who is good (God) covered the first four. His references to commandments 5, 6, 7, 8, and 9 can all be summed up by "Love your neighbor as yourself." Notice that He failed to mention commandment number 10, "Do not covet." I wonder why. Jesus' answer disappointed the young man, because he regarded it as too simple. He had followed the commandments perfectly, or so he thought. Yet he still had not secured peace of mind or the certainty of his salvation.

GROUP DISCUSSION

1. What clues from this story lead you to believe the young man came to Jesus with an honest and sincere request?

2. Do you know people who believe that God grants eternal life based on the satisfactory performance of particular religious or benevolent acts?

3. In talking with people about eternal life, what percent of them have you found who believe they're going to heaven? What percent of them believe they're going to hell?

4. Why did Jesus place so much emphasis in His ministry on loving one's neighbors as oneself?

READ MATT. 19:21-22

Notice that Jesus gave the requirement for the young man to be perfect. We studied Jesus' call to perfection in Book 2, Study 1, as we looked at Matt. 5:48. Here we see that Jesus made a specific prescription for reaching this standard. The young man must deal with his internal problem of covetousness (Commandment 10) by outwardly letting go of the material possessions he loved most. His possessions defined him; people spoke of him in terms of his great wealth. So he needed to let go of these possessions that blocked a clear path to God.

Bible scholars agree that Jesus' advice to this young man does not apply equally to all believers. In other words, Jesus was not condemning material possessions or salaried employment. Jesus simply requires us to remove all stumbling blocks that stand between us and fellowship with God and His will for our lives.

Look past Jesus' call to conduct a garage sale and give the profits to poor people who could not pay the young man back or boost his social standing. Why did Jesus require this level of commitment? Our answer lies in the last phrase of Jesus' command: "Come, follow me." That says it all! That's the same command and call to reckless abandon of personal ambitions that Jesus gave His disciples. They cast everything aside to follow Him. His command remains the same for us today.

GROUP DISCUSSION

1. Why do people let their possessions own them?

2. Why do people let others define them by their level of wealth, status, or material prosperity?

3. What other stumbling blocks stand between people and fellowship with God and His will for their lives?

4. What percent of our personal ambitions must we give to Jesus in order to be His disciple?

5. Why does discipleship with Jesus require total commitment?

A mind-set of service and ministry requires us to remove all stumbling blocks that stand between us and fellowship with God and His will for our lives. We must keep a light touch on our possessions, social status, desires, ambitions, and goals in life. We must adopt God's perspective for self-denial. The young man in this story needed to let go of wealth, the trinkets it purchased, and the status it earned him within his community. Once he realized the price tag of discipleship with Jesus, he walked away from the deal.

Apparently the price was too high for him. It was an amazing realization for a man who had the power to buy anything regardless of the price. Jesus required something of the young man he couldn't afford. Ironic isn't it? The very thing to which he clung tightly for security and satisfaction cost him his eternal life!

We read this story and think, *How sad!* Before we judge the young man too quickly, however, we should ask ourselves, *Does this story offer me a warning as well?* Absolutely. We've talked in this Bible study about giving God everything and consecrating ourselves completely to Him. We've talked about living *in* the world but not *of* it. We've talked about living as a sacrifice to God. We've talked about complete devotion to His cause. All of these concepts sound admirable and deeply spiritual. We know the ideas, but can we make the application to our daily lives? Can we find practical ways to put feet to our good intentions?

We, too, must watch for subtle stumbling blocks to our spiritual commitment. These include anything that means more to us than pleasing God completely. Such obstacles make us weak and ineffective in our commitment to Christ, because they divide that commitment. Once we remove them, we clear the path to a life of service and ministry for the cause of Christ.

PERSONAL REFLECTION

1. What has your commitment to Christ required you to keep a light touch on in your life?

2. Are you willing to surrender all your possessions, social status, desires, ambitions, and goals in life for the cause of Christ?

3. Are you open to a life of service and ministry for His kingdom?

FOR FURTHER STUDY

Matt. 16:24

Col. 3:14

James 2:22

Take a moment at the conclusion of the session to encour-

FURTHER QUESTIONS

age class participants to place their unanswered questions on note cards, along with this session number. They should then place their cards in an "odds and ends" box provided by the Bible study leader. Attention will be given to these questions in the last session of this study.

Investing in the Kingdom

Matt. 25:31-40

Uncle Clyde and Aunt Stella operated a rice farm two hours south of the farm I grew up on. Everyone in the community knew them for their Christian witness. As Christians, they attended church regularly and exemplified Christian lifestyles, but that's not what gave them notoriety in the community. Most folks, both Christians and not-yet Christians, knew them for their incredible benevolence. God prospered them materially, and they used their good fortune to reach out and bless others. I've never known anyone who applied this week's passage of Scripture as literally as my aunt and uncle.

I hate to even begin to give examples of their benevolence, because it took so many forms. Aunt Stella knitted a blanket for every mother who had a baby within driving distance of her house. She made a quilt by hand for every newlywed couple she knew. Sue and I cherish the one she gave us 30 years ago. She quilted long after she went blind and nearly until she died at the age of 96. Uncle Clyde quietly slipped money into the hands of persons going through difficult times. He grew a garden three times the size he needed for his own family so he could give vegetables away to people in need. Everyone in the community felt welcome to help themselves to anything in that garden.

If you asked them what motivated them to live such benevolent lives, I'm not sure they would know what you were talking about. Their lifestyle flowed so naturally from their love for Christ that it seemed like the only thing to do. Christ obviously meant the world to them, so they spent their lives passing on the blessings they received from Him.

GROUP DISCUSSION

1. Have you ever known someone like Uncle Clyde and Aunt Stella?

2. What was it about this person's lifestyle that impressed you, and why?

3. Why does this kind of person impress you so much?

READ MATT. 25:31-34

Jesus describes in this passage the final judgment of humanity at the end of time. "All the nations" indicates that both believers and nonbelievers stand before the judgment seat of God to hear His verdict on their lives. Jesus references the common practice of shepherds grazing sheep and goats together in the daytime and separating them at night.

The right hand signified a place of honor, the left a place of dishonor. This differentiation held true not only in biblical writing but in popular literature of the day as well. Jesus' listeners quickly identified with His images. The Judge first calls out those on His right to come into His kingdom. They leave their daily toil, temptation, stress, and labor for the heavenly bliss of God's presence. They receive their inheritance—that for which they have longed and waited. They now become citizens of the kingdom of heaven.

Notice how long God has been planning and working toward that day: since the creation of the world. In other words, He's had this day in mind since before Adam and Eve walked away from His plan in the garden. Like a proud parent planning a homecoming celebration for a child for many long years, God extends His hands and says with a beaming smile, "Welcome home."

GROUP DISCUSSION

1. Should stories about Judgment Day, like the one Jesus tells here, frighten or excite Christians?

2. What do you most look forward to *ending* on that day?

3. What do you most look forward to *beginning* on that day?

4. What will you enjoy most about the inheritance that God will give you on that day?

READ MATT. 25:35-36

We must always remember that salvation comes our way as a gift of God's grace and mercy. We don't earn or deserve it. Paul says in Eph. 2:8-9, "It is by grace you have been saved, through faith—and this not from yourselves, it is the gift of God—not by works, so that no one can boast." So we must never interpret Jesus' words to mean we earn our salvation through acts of benevolence. No one purchases heaven through deeds.

Jesus focuses attention not on the benevolent deeds but

on the attitudes and the conditions of the hearts of the people who do those deeds. He does not list a single roster of acts that He approves. His list merely illustrates the types of deeds people do when they have God-pleasing hearts and attitudes.

What does Jesus imply about the hearts and attitudes of the people who do the deeds mentioned in verses 35-36? They deny themselves in order to assist others. Their hearts are filled with devotion to others and self-sacrifice. They go out of their way and so open their homes to others. Their hearts are filled with sympathy and compassion. They genuinely care about the physical and emotional needs of others. They give of themselves as well as their material possessions. They view no task as too menial or beneath them. The love of God flows from their hearts into their deeds.

PERSONAL REFLECTION

1. At what qualities mentioned by Jesus do you excel?

2. To what qualities do you need to give more attention?

3. Take a moment to ask God to help you value the things He values and to give you a heart that pleases Him.

So often when we think of doing good deeds, our attention focuses on accomplishments or achievements. Notice that Jesus does not call attention to goals reached; He emphasizes the effort of the deeds no matter how small they seem. It's a simple act to offer a drink of water. Yet Jesus lifts such expressions of kindness to special divine favor. Notice,

too, that the sick do not necessarily become well or the imprisoned necessarily go free as a result of our efforts. That's
probably not within our power. He asks only that we do what
we can. Rather than feeling guilty for not being able to do
everything, we should concentrate on doing the few things
that we can do. Jesus highlights simple deeds that everyone
can do to manifest God's love to a needy world.

GROUP DISCUSSION

1. Why do we tend to emphasize accomplishments or
   achievements rather than intentions?

2. Why does Jesus not call attention to accomplishments?

3. Why does Jesus give such favor to such simple deeds?

READ MATT. 25:37-40

Like my aunt and uncle, the righteous seem surprised at
God's favor with their simple deeds done in His name and
with His love. Their hearts fill with humility as they admit that
they only passed along a small measure of what they received from God in great measure. They did their benevolent
acts with such self-denial that God's attention to those acts
overwhelms them. They weren't aware at the time that God
even noticed them. So they certainly did not expect to be re-
warded for them.

One of the most profound insights into the entire gospel

story occurs in verse 40. Here we learn just how completely Jesus identifies with those who suffer and are needy. He identifies so closely that He feels their suffering and our comfort given to those who suffer. Amazing!

GROUP ACTIVITY

Give each class member three note cards. Read the following statement to the class: "Jesus began a list of benevolent acts significant in God's eyes. What deeds can you add to this list that will please God? Write your responses on note cards." When all have finished their responses, collect the cards and read them aloud. You may want to print the list and distribute it to the class next week.

FOR FURTHER STUDY

Deut. 10:12

1 Sam. 15:22

John 21:17

FURTHER QUESTIONS

Take a moment at the conclusion of the session to encourage class participants to place their unanswered questions on note cards, along with this session number. They should then place their cards in an "odds and ends" box provided by the Bible study leader. Attention will be given to these questions in the last session of this study.

Your Unconscious Influence

Mark 5:22-36

Several years ago someone made a comment to me in passing that got me to thinking about an area of ministry we seldom acknowledge. The encounter went something like this. The person said, "I notice you and Brent [my son] have a strong bond and a good relationship."

I asked, "How do you know that?"

He said, "For some time now, I've been watching from a distance the interaction between you two. I've studied the way you talk to each other, your body language when you're together, and the way you respond to one another. Your relationship has been an encouragement to me."

That conversation spooked me a bit, because it reminded me that, like it or not, people are watching my life. They notice the way I act and react. They listen to what I say and to what I really mean. They see the way I treat others. They even observe the way I drive. As hard as I might try, I can't spot them in the crowd. But they're there nonetheless. In this Bible study we'll explore together the ministry of our unconscious influence.

GROUP DISCUSSION

1. Do you ever think about the fact that people both within and outside the Church are watching your life?

2. How does that make you feel?

READ MARK 5:22-36

Mark 5:22-36 relates a story within a story. The first story begins by telling us about Jarius's sick daughter and Jesus' intervention to heal her. The second story takes place as Jesus and His disciples travel to Jarius's home. We want to focus our attention on the second story about the sick woman. This second story offers many insights about such things as

- the kindness and compassion of Jesus for a terribly ill person;
- the miraculous power of Jesus' physical presence;
- the connection between spiritual and physical life;
- the rewards of simple faith.

However, as we study the story of the sick woman, I want to view it from the perspective of the ministry of Jesus' unconscious influence. For the sake of our discussion, let's not debate the question of whether Jesus had foreknowledge of this particular woman's presence in the crowd prior to her approach. Since He is God, in all likelihood He could have had an awareness of her presence. Put yourself in Jesus' sandals and imagine how you might have assessed the situation.

GROUP DISCUSSION

1. What do you learn about Jesus' heart from the kindness and compassion He showed toward a terribly ill person?

2. Give examples of the way our spiritual lives affect our physical lives and vice versa.

3. Why does God so quickly and willingly reward simple faith?

Notice first of all in this story that the sick woman probably had her eye on Jesus' life and ministry for a long time. She may have stood in the shadows numerous times as Jesus preached to the crowds and healed the sick people who approached Him in faith. She saw His mercy, love, and compassion toward the sick and needy. She imagined herself going up to Him and receiving a miracle of physical healing just as so many others had received. She played that imaginative encounter over and over in her mind, wishing again and again that it might become a reality. This woman's silent examination of Jesus and His impact on her life reminds us of our own unconscious influence on those who watch our lives.

PERSONAL REFLECTION

Think about the fact that people are standing in the shadows watching your life. How then should you live?

Next, notice that the woman reaches out and touches Jesus at a time when He's extremely busy and preoccupied. He's thinking about Jarius's daughter; He needs to reach her quickly. Every second counts. He doesn't really have time to deal with another person right at that moment. And yet this sick woman interrupts Him.

The way Jesus handles this situation reminds us of the importance of watching for ministry opportunities in the interruptions of our lives. Often we see these interruptions as hindrances working against progress toward our goals. We can interpret these interruptions as obstacles to be overcome rather than opportunities for reaching out to needy people. Remember your unconscious influence during times of interruption.

GROUP DISCUSSION

1. How do you view interruptions when you're extremely busy and preoccupied, as Jesus found himself that day?

2. How do you shift your thinking to view these interruptions as ministry opportunities rather than hindrances working against progress toward your goals?

3. Share personal examples of ministry opportunities you've discovered in the interruptions of your life.

Further notice that this incident happened at a time when Jesus was being hard pressed by the large crowd. Verse 24 says that the large crowd not only followed Him but also pressed around Him. The King James Version says the people thronged Him. In other words, they got into His personal space and inconvenienced Him.

So often the interruptions in our lives occur at the worst possible times. But then, honestly, when do we ever anxiously await an interruption? This story reminds us that Jesus lived with stress and out-of-control schedules just as we do. He knew what it meant to have too many entries on His daily calendar. He also knew what it meant to be pushed and shoved by the crowd while at the same time being hit up for a healing. "One thing at a time, please!" How many times have you said that?

Look at the poise and composure of Jesus as He stops His trip to Jarius's house and addresses this poor woman's need. Let His example encourage us to approach our interruptions that often occur at the worst possible times with the same poise and composure. Life seldom tosses challenges our way one at a time. They usually come in herds! Remember your unconscious influence during those "worst possible times."

GROUP DISCUSSION

1. Why do you suppose our interruptions often occur at the worst possible times?

2. How can we display the same poise and composure that Jesus displayed when too many things come at us at once?

3. What have you discovered helps control your stress best when too many things come at you at once?

Jesus further reminds us that ministry to others takes something out of us. We've talked a great deal in this Bible study series about dedicating ourselves fully to God and allowing Him to use us to reach out to others. While we acknowledge the importance of that availability to God, we must also remember that such giving of ourselves takes something from us. Jesus had such an awareness of the spiritual component of His earthly life that He immediately recognized that even His unconscious influence was costing Him something.

We seldom acknowledge the fact that our ministry to others takes physical and spiritual energy from us. That means we must balance the inflow and outflow. That is, recognize the need to draw away and restore our physical and spiritual batteries after a time of self-giving in ministry. This is an absolutely essential principle of Christian discipleship. Otherwise, we risk the damaging effects of burnout. Too many Christians have fallen along the way because they failed to heed the principle of inflow and outflow. Remember the draining effect even on your unconscious influence.

PERSONAL REFLECTION

1. How conscious are you of the draining effect of ministering to others?

2. In what ways do you guard your life against burnout?

3. How do you balance the inflow and outflow of your life?

GROUP ACTIVITY

This study emphasized our unconscious influence. Give each member of your Bible study group a lump of Play-Doh. Have each person mold something that will serve as a reminder that others are watching his or her life. Give everyone an opportunity to share the spiritual insight of his or her symbol.

FOR FURTHER STUDY

Mark 4:35-41

John 6:4-13

Acts 27:13-26

FURTHER QUESTIONS

Take a moment at the conclusion of the session to encourage class participants to place their unanswered questions on note cards, along with this session number. They should then place their cards in an "odds and ends" box provided by the Bible study leader. Attention will be given to these questions in the last session of this study.

Offering Deliverance

Luke 4:16-21

Things aren't always as they appear. Our son Brent's best friend, David, possesses the unusual ability to imitate a variety of accents. He can convincingly impersonate just about anyone over the phone. He's fooled me more than once. Over a period of time his friends have learned to doubt the authenticity of any caller they're not absolutely certain about. They're always suspicious that it might be David tricking them again.

People in Jesus' day spent their entire lives looking and waiting for the promised Messiah. Every Jewish mother hoped her newborn son might be God's choice for their deliverer. Imposters had fooled the people across the years with false claims to the point that they weren't very receptive any longer. They had been disappointed too many times. They had learned to doubt the authenticity of anyone who made declarations of messiahship.

That's the mind-set Jesus faced in this week's passage of scripture. He may have had hometown advantage, but it didn't help Him in this situation. The people were not as open to Jesus' ministry as one might expect.

GROUP DISCUSSION

1. Have you learned to doubt certain things in life such as advertising hype, product claims, and slight-of-hand magicians?

2. What led you to such doubt?

3. What would it take to change your mind about such matters?

READ LUKE 4:16-17

The community gathered weekly at the synagogue to hear scripture read. Common practice offered visitors and guests the opportunity to read the scripture passage. The event we study in Luke 4:16-17 happened perhaps a year into Jesus' public ministry. He had a good reputation in the community in which He had grown up, so it seemed natural to ask Him to read. Readers always read one passage from the Law (the first five books of the Old Testament) and another from the Prophets (any of the Old Testament prophets). The first passage was preselected; the reader could choose his second reading.

At this point in the story, listeners had an open mind about Jesus and His message. Reports of His ministry in surrounding villages seemed positive enough, and the home crowd eagerly awaited the scripture reading.

PERSONAL REFLECTION

Think of a time in your life when the spotlight was on you as you performed. What thoughts were in your mind with regard to such matters as

- wanting to do your best?
- wanting to make a good impression?
- wanting to help your listeners?

READ LUKE 4:18-21

Jesus read Isa. 61:1-2. This passage immediately calls attention to the Hebrew people returning from captivity. However, their return did not fulfill everything highlighted in the text. So God meant for us to glean more from the passage than only insight regarding Hebrew captivity. Jesus told His hearers that this passage applied to His ministry as well. In fact, He told them that Isaiah wrote it about *His own* ministry. Now there's a mouthful!

Jesus ministered in a particularly difficult time in human history. His people lived with extreme poverty and oppression. Discontent and discord prevailed. Rome totally subjugated the Hebrew people, and as most folks saw it, only a political revolution would help them. No one but the Messiah could bring deliverance.

Jesus startled His listeners when He announced that He fulfilled this prophecy. In fact, He had been sent by God as the One they had long awaited. Their prayers had been answered—deliverance was coming.

GROUP DISCUSSION

1. Do you see any connection between the bondage and oppression people experience in our day compared with that of Jesus' day?

2. Is this ministry of Jesus still needed in our day?

3. Who will carry on His ministry in our world?

Jesus left us with instructions to carry on His ministry when He went back to heaven (John 14:12). He promised to be with us (John 14:18; Heb. 13:5); He promised to empower our actions (Acts 1:8). In this week's passage of scripture, Jesus details the goals of His ministry. Thus, He presents us with a plan to continue what He started. He emphasizes the fact that the Holy Spirit empowered His activity by anointing Him. The same Spirit is essential to the success of our efforts as well.

Jesus lists five activities from Isaiah's prophesy that characterize His ministry; He thereby gives instruction regarding the direction His followers should take His ministry once He leaves it with them:

- A ministry to the poor.
- A ministry of freedom to prisoners.
- A ministry of sight to the blind.
- A ministry of release to the oppressed.
- A ministry of the Lord's favor.

The last phrase gives definition to the others. It references the Year of Jubilee (Lev. 25:8-55). Every 50 years all slaves received their freedom, all loans were marked "paid in full," and all property returned to its original owners. Jesus interprets Isaiah's words to refer also to His offer of salvation from sin. Every year can be a Year of Jubilee when Jesus brings liberation and deliverance.

GROUP DISCUSSION

1. In what ways can people be poor besides lacking adequate money?

2. In what ways can people be imprisoned besides being confined to jail?

3. In what ways can people be blind other than physically?

4. In what ways can people be oppressed besides suffering political bondage?

GROUP ACTIVITY

Divide your class into four small groups. Ask each group to brainstorm answers to the following question regarding one of the following: poverty, imprisonment, blindness, oppression. "In what ways can you and your fellowship of believers continue Jesus' ministry of deliverance to people living with this type of suffering?"

CONCLUSION

At the conclusion of Luke's account of Jesus' hometown synagogue scripture reading, he reports that the townspeople did not receive Jesus and His message well. They rejected him as an imposter such as we discussed in the introduction. Jesus did not match their preconceived notions of the Messiah, so they dismissed His claims as false and drove Him from His hometown. We must learn from Jesus even in this strange turn of events. He has called us to follow Him. We must follow whether the path is easy or hard, whether we're accepted or rejected.

GROUP DISCUSSION

1. Did Jesus discontinue His ministry after the people of His hometown rejected Him? Why not?

2. Should you discontinue your ministry if some people refuse your help or reject your attempts to offer deliverance?

FURTHER QUESTIONS

Take a moment at the conclusion of the session to encourage class participants to place their unanswered questions on note cards, along with this session number. They should then place their cards in an "odds and ends" box provided by the Bible study leader. Attention will be given to these questions in the last session of this study.

Sharing My Faith

1 Pet. 3:15-16; John 9:25

Growing up on a farm afforded me many opportunities for adventures the city kids simply did not have. How many city kids can say their dad dug into a dinosaur skeleton? Archeologists from the state university came and carefully unearthed it for research. How many city kids regularly watch for rattlesnakes, three-foot-long snapping turtles, and wolves as they walk near their homes? We even had an otter come around once!

My point? Farm kids can talk about dogs, cats, cows, horses, pigs, and every other "normal" animal all day long. Nobody's impressed. But throw in an exciting adventure with an otter or a snapping turtle, and ears perk up. I had a story for every animal I ever encountered on our farm. I can't begin to count how many people I told about the dinosaur. You had better believe I told everyone who would listen and was willing to look at my pictures.

It's not hard to narrate a personal experience. You just tell what you saw or what happened. Observers of car accidents or tornadoes do it every night on the evening news. Many television stations call their news programs "Eyewitness News." They present the evening news through the testimony of eyewitnesses who give firsthand accounts of what they saw or experienced.

GROUP DISCUSSION

1. What's the most exciting personal experience that's happened in your life?

2. How many people did you tell about it?

3. Did your story change dramatically from one time you told it to another, or did you just relate the facts and main points every time you told it?

READ 1 PET. 3:15-16

In 1 Pet. 3:15-26, Peter tells us to set Christ apart as Lord in our hearts. The original language says it as "sanctify the Christ as Lord." Peter's appeal, which he takes from Isa. 8:13, is blasphemy if Jesus Christ is not God. He urges us to regard Christ as holy and serve Him in reverence and awe. As Jesus taught us in the Lord's Prayer (Matt. 6:9-13), we're to reverence or hallow God's name. This attitude toward God should flow from our inner being.

Once we give Christ His proper place in our hearts, we then prepare a personal testimony to share with others about our faith. Peter's direction here does not demand memorizing a theological defense of the Christian religion. Rather, he's talking about telling our own salvation story in our own words. We should think through our responses to such questions as

- How did you come to know the Lord as your personal Savior?
- In your own words, who is Jesus Christ?
- Why are you a Christian?
- What does faith and Jesus mean to you?
- How do you cope when the troubles of life close in on you?
- Why do you have such a positive outlook on life?
- Where is your hope?

PERSONAL REFLECTION

1. Have you thought through your personal answers to these questions? If not, take time over the next few days to do so.

2. What are the main elements that should be included in everyone's presentation?

We are advised to think through our personal statement, because it's important to always be ready to give a concise, well-reasoned response when asked about our Christian hope, as Peter calls it. We speak up for two important reasons: (1) we want to defend God's truth, and (2) we want to impart understanding to those who hear us, understanding that will hopefully lead to their salvation. Our presentation must be simple and personal.

Peter also says we must make our presentation with gentleness and respect. It's better to say nothing than to speak up for Christ with a spirit of arrogance or superiority. A tone of judgment or condemnation must never be detected in our testimonies. We actually approach the subject from an attitude of weakness and dependence upon God's Spirit for the correct words to speak. Few Christians feel adequate for the task. That's good, because it helps us depend more on God's strength and wisdom than on our own.

GROUP DISCUSSION

1. Why must our presentation be simple and personal?

2. Why must we make our presentation with gentleness and respect?

3. What are some words or concepts to avoid completely in our presentation?

4. How does depending upon God help us and our presentation?

Peter goes on to remind us of the importance of keeping a clear conscience. Paul also speaks often of keeping a clear conscience (See 1 Tim. 1:5; 1 Cor. 4:4.). This enables us to *live* our lives to match up with what we *say* about our faith in God. Anyone can memorize a powerful salvation story and tell it to all who will listen. However, if the testimony of the person's life does not demonstrate what he or she says, the cause of Christ is hurt more than it's helped.

Our good conduct should be transparent for all to see. In this way, those who might speak against us will be ashamed of their untruthful words. Even if someone chooses to say such things about us, others will not listen to or believe him or her. They can see for themselves that our lives show otherwise.

GROUP DISCUSSION

1. Why is it so important for our lives to match up with what we say about our faith in God?

2. How do we live transparent lives for all to see our good conduct?

3. What is your best defense against those who might speak against you?

READ JOHN 9:25

Peter talks in our previous passage about sharing our personal testimony. The man in John 9:25 actually puts Peter's words into practice. He offers us an example to follow. Jesus heals the man in the early part of chapter 9. The Pharisees gather to investigate the incident because they believe Jesus violated their laws with this healing. The man's parents refuse to involve themselves in the inquiry, because they fear they'll lose worship privileges at the Temple. They insist that their son speak for himself. After asked a number of leading questions on two separate occasions, he gives the powerful testimony we find in our text.

Notice that the healed man refuses to get caught up in theological arguments. He knows how fruitless such arguments are. He refuses to side with the Pharisees—yet he refuses to remain silent. He does what we can all do—he simply tells his personal experience in his own words. His testimony has no drama and very little detail. But it hit the central message of Jesus' touch! I love the way he cut through all the intellectual gymnastics of the Pharisees with his simple statement: "I was blind but now I see!"

GROUP DISCUSSION

1. Why should we seek to avoid theological arguments when we share our faith?

2. Why is it that God can powerfully use a testimony of our personal experience in our own words?

3. Why is it important to talk about Jesus' touch in our lives?

CONCLUSION

I began this study talking about the stories of adventure from my childhood. Did you make the connection between the introduction and the rest of the Bible study? The story of Christ's work in our lives is too exciting not to tell! We don't have to be effervescent and dramatic—we just have to be real. People care more about our being genuine than they do about hearing a grandiose tale.

Sharing our personal stories about Jesus and our hope in Him is an important element in living lives of holiness.

GROUP ACTIVITY

Give class members each a sheet of paper. Ask them to write down the main points of their spiritual journeys with God. After everyone completes the assignment, divide the class into pairs. Encourage all to share their stories with their partners. Then encourage all members of the class to share their stories this week with at least one friend who does not know Christ.

FOR FURTHER STUDY

2 Tim. 1:8; 2:21

Mark 5:18-19

Acts 1:8

FURTHER QUESTIONS

Take a moment at the conclusion of the session to encourage class participants to place their unanswered questions on note cards, along with this session number. They should then place their cards in an "odds and ends" box provided by the Bible study leader. Attention will be given to these questions in the last session of this study.

Making Disciples

Matt. 28:16-20

"It takes a village to raise a child." That idea, popularized in the 1990s, received a great deal of both positive and negative national attention. I mention it here not to begin another discussion about public education, child welfare, or health care. I want to spin it a bit to suggest an important principle of Christian faith: "It takes a church to raise a disciple."

As we discussed in Book 3, the normal path of Christian discipleship is not a solitary one. An entire Christian community walks the path together, aiding and supporting one another along the way. Christian discipleship is never just a "Jesus and me" venture. It includes the input of every member of Christ's Body on this earth. This week's Bible study passage reminds us that each of us has a part to play in bringing the not-yet believers into Christ's fold. In the 10 studies that precede this one, we have focused on both mind-sets for service and actual ministries to which God calls us. This week's study reminds us of one of the most important ministries to which God invites us to join Him.

GROUP DISCUSSION

1. What comes to mind when you hear, "It takes a church to raise a disciple"?

2. Do you feel a personal responsibility in this challenge?

3. If so, is it a vague feeling of responsibility, or is it a specific feeling of responsibility? ("I ought to do *something*" versus "I ought to do *this thing*.")

READ MATT. 28:16-20

The event described in Matt. 28:16-20 occurred at the end of Jesus' time on earth following His resurrection. The context of the passage seems to indicate that the 11 apostles of Jesus, along with other followers, heard Him deliver this challenge. Matthew records for us this first time that His disciples fully worshiped Him as their God.

An interesting aside to this story reminds us that even Christ himself, with loving disciples bowing at His feet in worship, had followers who stood around the edges of the scene and doubted. We can't neglect the ministry God calls us to do for Him just because some people stand around the edges, criticizing our efforts. Doubters and critics surface just about everywhere.

In this closing account in Matthew's gospel Jesus does at least three things. He declares His ultimate authority (verse 18). He commissions His apostles and us to spread the gospel message and make disciples (vv. 19-20). He promises to be with us every day of our lives (v. 20).

GROUP DISCUSSION

1. What finally convinced Jesus' disciples that He is God so that here, for the first time, they fully worshiped Him as God?

2. If we're not to neglect the ministry God calls us to do just because some people criticize our efforts, how should we regard their criticism and doubt?

3. Why do you suppose Jesus got His followers together one more time to talk with them as a group?

Verse 18 offers us a brief glimpse into a heavenly transaction. In ways we will never understand this side of eternity, Jesus' coming to our earth, His death, and His resurrection earned Him all authority in all of God's creation. The Son of God received this authority from the Father. A new contract between God and humanity took effect. God opened a new way to salvation for all humanity in this transaction. Our adventure story with God can be a reality because the Father granted this authority to His Son.

PERSONAL REFLECTION

How does it make you feel to realize that the Father, Son, and Holy Spirit went to so much effort to implement a new contract for you?

In verse 19 Jesus shares some of His authority with His disciples. This includes not only the disciples present with Jesus that day but all disciples of Jesus who follow after, including us. In essence, Jesus deputizes us to participate with Him in getting the word out about this new contract with God. Here, then, we receive our commission to join Jesus in disciple-making. This commission includes us all.

We looked at the various roles God assigns to His followers in the Christian community in Book 3, Study 1: apostles, prophets, evangelists, pastors, and teachers (Eph. 4:11). Paul lists many other roles in 1 Cor. 12:7-11 and Rom. 12:6-8. These varying roles differ among us based on our different gifts, talents, abilities, and personalities. God uses each of us in our own unique way to contribute to the growth and development of His kingdom. That's why in 1 Cor. 12:12-31 Paul takes extra effort to explain the importance of recognizing and coordinating our various strengths and weaknesses.

In our Scripture passage for this week, however, Jesus gives a commission to all of us. He does not reserve disciple-making only for preachers or evangelists. He challenges us all. We are to

- go
- make disciples in all nations
- baptize them into faith
- teach them the doctrines and lifestyle for Christ's followers.

GROUP DISCUSSION

1. How do you personalize Jesus' command to "go"?

2. What all is involved in making a Christian disciple?

3. What role do you play in disciple-making?

In the last part of verse 20, Jesus promises to be with us. Matthew begins and ends his book with this reminder. He begins in 1:23 by calling Mary's child "Immanuel," which means "God with us." We imply that to reference Jesus coming to earth to live among us. In 28:20 Jesus extends His presence to us even after He returns to heaven. He promises to remain by our sides for as long as we live. He fulfilled that promise by sending us the Holy Spirit (John 14:18 and Acts 2:1-4).

Jesus charges every word in this passage with an urgent challenge. Notice how He balances His great challenge to go into all the world and make disciples with a great promise to boost our courage. We don't go out to the nations alone. We don't devise our own plans. We don't create our own strategies. With the aid of the Holy Spirit, we face the challenge to make disciples by receiving direction and strength from Christ himself! He's our Companion, Guide, Confidant, and Friend. Partnering together with the Creator of the universe to make disciples for His kingdom—what a challenge!

His promise to be at our side applies not just to our difficult days or our heavy ministry days—it applies to our every day as well. Sure, you expect God to draw near to you when you're tempted, tried, persecuted, or challenged as a result of your faith. But Jesus says He'll be with you on your great days and even your ordinary, run-of-the-mill days. Now that's a Friend who sticks by your side closer than a brother or sister! He'll be with you right until you cross over to the other side; then He'll welcome you across the threshold of heaven's door.

GROUP DISCUSSION

1. What encourages you most about Jesus' promise?

2. Why does Jesus so carefully balance His great challenge to go into all the world and make disciples with a promise to boost our courage?

3. What encouragement do you receive from this reminder that Jesus is with you every day of your life?

GROUP ACTIVITY

Put the words "Go," "Make disciples," "Baptize," and "Teach" in large letters across the top of a chalkboard or dry-erase board at the front of the classroom. Give class members four Post-it notes each. Ask them to suggest the reason Jesus asked us to do each of these things. Instruct them to write their answers. When everyone has finished, have class members stick their notes under the words on the board to which they apply. The class leader should read all the responses.

FOR FURTHER STUDY

John 5:27

Col. 1:15-20

Isa. 43:2

FURTHER QUESTIONS

Take a moment at the conclusion of the session to encourage class participants to place their unanswered questions on note cards, along with this session number. They should then place their cards in an "odds and ends" box provided by the Bible study leader. Attention will be given to these questions in the last session of this study.

Tying It All Together

In Book 4 we've explored "Serving Others Along the Road." We've talked about taking our consecrated, changed lives to the streets as we involve ourselves in service and ministry to our troubled world. We live in a community of faith and a needy world. Our commitment to Christ thrusts us into both service and ministry.

Rather than allowing us to escape to ease and comfort, Jesus sends us right into the frontline of the battle, where people need us most. Part of our discussion has involved approaching the task in a good attitude; the rest of the challenge involves actually *doing* something. We sometimes refer to holiness as "perfect love." This love that God places in our hearts reveals itself in the way we live our lives. Our actions are seldom dramatic or newsworthy. Usually they're small, insignificant to many, and unnoticed by most. But God sees them, and in His own special way He uses them to help needy people and to build His kingdom.

GROUP ACTIVITY

Bible study participants have been encouraged throughout this study to place their unanswered questions on note cards in the "odds and ends" box. Use time at the beginning of this session to consider these questions in the form of a group discussion. The Bible study leader should add clarity wherever necessary and draw each question, with answers, to a close. It is possible that more time will be needed to adequately address lingering questions than one study session can accommodate. In that case, plan ahead to make this study a two-part session. It's important that all previous questions be answered before moving on to a final wrap-up of the study material.

READ JOHN 17:14-16

Jesus calls us to maintain a tricky balance between personal interests or activities and the world. He tells us to work, play, and minister in our world but cautions us against allowing the world to control our thinking or value system. On the surface we probably look like any other citizen of this world, but the motivation and spirit of our lives are different. We live in the light of God's truth, and that places us in dramatic contrast to the darkness of sin's bondage that surrounds us.

Jesus forgives us of our sins and sanctifies our hearts not to place us on a fireplace mantle like a treasured trophy. Rather, He cleans us up and screws our heads on straight so we can go out and offer God's comfort. He comforts us not to make us comfortable but to make us comforters.

GROUP DISCUSSION

Now that you've had several weeks to think about it, how would you explain to a new Christian Jesus' call to live *in* the world but not to be *of* the world?

READ MATT. 5:13-16

Jesus used comparisons to such things as salt, light, and yeast to describe our places in the world in which we live and serve. Paul says that we're to live as sacrifices to God. Living as He has called us requires a radical departure from our comfort zones. Those who heed the call to be salt, light, yeast, and to live a life of sacrifice stand out in a crowd. They don't function like others around them. They make a difference because they *are* different. They *influence* for good—with a far greater reach than their mere efforts. They bring out the best in others and the situations in which they find themselves. The world is a better place because of their presence and their efforts.

GROUP DISCUSSION

What does the call to be salt, light, yeast, and a living sacrifice say to you about the attitude you take into your daily life of service to God in your world?

READ MATT. 13:44-46

Jesus tells two stories that call us to take risks for God. He wants us, of all things, to concentrate all our efforts and energy in life on a single purpose. In other words, He calls us to single-minded dedication toward God's kingdom. That has serious ramifications about how we spend our time and money. It means we focus every ounce of our energy, every minute of every day, and every dime that comes our way on Kingdom priorities.

GROUP DISCUSSION

In what ways does Jesus illustrate your life and spiritual priorities as He tells these two stories?

READ 2 COR. 12:7-10

Service and ministry for the cause of Christ don't exempt you from difficulties in life. Rain falls on the just and the unjust alike. Yet difficulties in the lives of believers differ greatly from those of nonbelievers because of the ways God works through us and uses our difficulties to make us stronger. He meets our weakness with His strength and builds His kingdom in the process.

Realizing this helps shape the way we approach weakness, hardships, and difficulties. If we allow Him, God can actually turn weaknesses, hardships, and difficulties into blessings for Christ's sake. We don't know how He does it; we just marvel that He does.

GROUP DISCUSSION

How might Paul's reminder relieve stress in the lives of believers who find themselves going through troubled times?

READ MATT. 19:21; 25:40

In Matt. 19:21 and 25:40 Jesus reminds us to establish mind-sets of service and ministry as we relate to our material possessions and financial resources. We must own our possessions rather than allowing them to own us. Further, we must find ways to invest our financial resources and possessions in Kingdom work. That investment can involve the simplest actions and efforts. God identifies himself so closely with suffering humanity that when we aid them, He feels it. We never know when our efforts make a Kingdom difference, so we make service and ministry a daily habit.

GROUP DISCUSSION

Now that you've had several weeks to think about it, how do you make your time and financial resources available for God's service on a daily basis?

READ MATT. 28:19-20

The last four Bible studies address various components of our Christian ministry. Matt. 28:19-20 reminds us of our responsibility to make disciples. That's a multifaceted task that requires all of us doing what God has called us to do best. As we all play our parts, people come to Christ, give their lives to Him, are adopted into the family of God, and find their places in the Body of Christ. From there, we incorporate them into the Christian community and help them become Christ's disciples. But evangelism and disciple-making are not the only ministries to which God calls us.

We all have a ministry of unconscious influence. We each play a role in offering deliverance to those in spiritual bondage. And we each have a story to tell of what Christ has done for us. These are not tasks we perform now and again. They are features that characterize our whole lifestyle. They're not just what we do; they're *who we are* as well. Whether you work in full-time Christian service or do secular work, every one plays a part in service and ministry for God's kingdom.

PERSONAL REFLECTION

What are your ministries for building God's kingdom?

FINAL GROUP ACTIVITY

Divide the class into pairs. Have the members in each pair share their responses with each other to the following questions. Then have one member of each pair share with the entire group the high points of their discussion.

1. What has been your greatest insight about "serving others along the road" from this Bible study?

2. What has been the hardest concept for you to grasp in this Bible study?

3. What is your favorite passage of scripture from this Bible study?

4. How has your life changed as a result of this Bible study?